JOB SURVIVAL SKILLS

by
MARGRET M. BREWNER
WILLIAM C. McMAHON
MICHAEL P. ROCHE

EDUCATIONAL DESIGN, INC.
EDI 325

ISBN# 0-87694-223-0   EDI 325

Table of Contents

When you enter the work world, getting a job can be a problem. But it's not always the biggest problem.

Holding on to the job is!

Many jobs are lost because the job holder didn't know or didn't understand the customs and demands of the work world. The work world requires you to have many skills in addition to the special skills you are hired for. These additional skills include being able to cooperate with other workers, using the telephone or dealing with the public courteously, communicating effectively, handling ordinary stress without going to pieces or flying off the handle, and many others.

We call these skills "Job Survival Skills." Without them, you won't survive on the job. You'll be fired, or you'll quit. Many are matters of ordinary courtesy, or good common sense. But many are special to the job world, which is more formal and guided by rules than is the world of, say, family or friendships.

This book will introduce you to many of the most important Job Survival Skills. You will learn many special rules and techniques involving personal appearance, positive attitudes, courtesy, initiative, dealing with others, and handling stress.

With these Job Survival Skills you will have a good chance of keeping the job you want, enjoying it, and moving ahead.

1. ATTENDANCE

One of the most important things an employer wants from an employee is good attendance. If you're not there, everyone else will have to work harder to get the job done.

You should always come to work unless you have a good reason not to. If you must miss work, however, follow these rules for notifying your boss:

1. **WHY**—Your reason for missing work had better be a good one. It should be a reason that your boss will accept.

2. **WHEN**—Whenever possible, if you are going to be absent, give your employer enough time to find someone to take your place.

3. **WHOM**—When you call in, make sure to talk to someone responsible—usually the person in charge of supervising your work. If you don't, your message may never reach your employer.

4. **HOW**—When you talk to your employer, your reason for missing work should be explained clearly, completely, and respectfully.

Sorry, Boss

Below are reasons why people miss work. Are they OK or POOR? Check one of the boxes next to each reason to show what you think. Then ask your employer or supervisor to check those she/he agrees with in the box under "Employer Agrees." If you are not employed, go to an employer or to anybody who has had to supervise other workers. Ask what he/she thinks.

I called in and said:	OK, if not done often	Poor Reason	Employer Agrees
1. "I'm sick in bed with the flu."	X		
2. "My child is sick."	X		
3. "I have a cold."	X		
4. "I missed the bus."		X	
5. "I can't find a baby-sitter."	X		
6. "We have relatives visiting this weekend."		X	
7. "There was a death in my family. I have to go to the funeral."	X		
8. "I just don't feel good."		X	
9. "My brother came home last night. I haven't seen him in a year. He's leaving tomorrow."		X	
10. "I have no way to get to work."		X	
11. "Someone I really like asked me out tonight."		X	
12. "I have to work on my car."		X	
13. "My husband/wife decided to go out of town today. I have to go along."		X	
14. "I have to go to the doctor's today."	X		
15. "I was up late last night. I'm too tired to go to work."		X	
16. "The bus passed me by at the bus stop."		X	
17. "My wife/husband and I had a fight last night."		X	

Why Do You Miss Work?

Some people rarely miss work. Others are absent fairly often. How often do you miss work (or school, if you go to school and don't have a job)?

Read the list below and check reasons that cause you to miss work or school fairly often —several times a year.

I miss work or school because

_____ 1. I am sick a lot.

_____ 2. I don't like the job (or school).

_____ 3. I have problems with the boss (or teachers).

_____ 4. I can't find a baby-sitter.

_____ 5. I have problems at home.

_____ 6. I am bored with the job (or school).

_____ 7. I'm not very good at my job (or at school).

_____ 8. I have trouble getting to work (or school).

_____ 9. I have too many other things I need to do.

_____ 10. I don't like the people I'm with.

_____ 11. I have trouble getting up in the morning.

_____ 12. My car keeps breaking down.

_____ 13. I have many jobs to do at home that keep me from going to work (or school).

_____ 14. I really don't know why I miss so much.

_____ 15. Other (Write out your reasons): _____

_____

_____

Look back over the items you checked. They tell you where you will want to improve in attendance.

Is My Timing Off?

You should give your employer as much notice as possible if you have to miss work.

If there is an emergency, call A.S.A.P. (As Soon As Possible). Even in an emergency, you can often give your employer three hours notice or more. This will give him/her a chance to find someone to replace you.

If there is some type of special occasion, you will almost always know about it in advance. Your employer will expect you to give notice of this kind of absence before the work schedule is made up. Most employers would expect to know two to three weeks in advance. Check to see how much notice your employer requires.

Below are some reasons for missing work. No matter how good the reason, the employer will be angry at you if you do not give him/her enough time to find someone to take your place. Look at the reasons below and decide if you could call in your reason the day of your absence, or if you would be expected to tell your boss one to two weeks in advance.

I called in and told my employer:	Same Day OK	1-2 Weeks Notice
1. "We're going on vacation."		
2. "I have a doctor's appointment."		
3. "I'm sick in bed with the flu."		
4. "My child is sick."		
5. "I have to help my brother move."		
6. "I have to go to court."		
7. "I broke my leg."		
8. "We have relatives coming in from out of town."		
9. "My brother came in unexpectedly last night. I haven't seen him in a year. He's leaving tomorrow."		
10. "I have to go to my daughter's graduation."		
11. "There was a death in my family. I have to go to the funeral."		
12. "I have a dentist's appointment."		
13. "Our family is going on a vacation."		
14. "We're going to a play."		
15. "My car broke down."		

16. "I have a date with someone I really like."		
17. "My Dad was just taken to the hospital."		
18. "I have a family get-together."		
19. "I have to pick up a friend at the airport."		

Below are situations in which employees might call explaining that they can't come to work. Pretend that you are an employee. Following the Rules Of Attendance, judge if the reason in each case is OK or POOR for missing work (in some cases you may just want to call to explain that you will be late). Circle what you think. Then explain WHEN you should call, WHOM you should talk with, and HOW you would explain your reason to the employer. Be sure your explanations are clear and polite. Don't be afraid to say you are sorry when an apology is in order.

1. Your car broke down late last night as you were returning from a movie. You had to have it towed to a garage 3 or 4 miles from your home. You want to spend the day getting it repaired. It is now 7 o'clock. You are supposed to start work at 9 A.M.

   WHY: OK/POOR

   WHEN: _____

   WHOM: _____

   HOW: _____

   _____

   _____

2. You woke up this morning with a bad headache and an upset stomach. Since you didn't have a fever, you hoped you would feel better. Instead you feel worse. It is now noon. You start work at 4 P.M.

   WHY: OK/POOR

   WHEN: _____

   WHOM: _____

   HOW: _____

   _____

   _____

3. You got up late and missed your bus. It is now 7:30 A.M. Another bus will not be along for an hour. You start work at 8:15 A.M.

   WHY: OK/POOR

   WHEN: _____

   WHOM: _____

   HOW: _____

   _____

   _____

4. You have a chance to go camping tomorrow with some friends. While you knew they were going to go a couple of weeks ago, you weren't sure you wanted to go with them until today.

WHY: OK/POOR

WHEN: _____

WHOM: _____

HOW: _____

_____

_____

5. Your baby-sitter called this morning and told you that she would not be able to come today. You've made a number of calls but couldn't find anyone to take her place. It is now 8 A.M. You start work at 9 A.M.

WHY: OK/POOR

WHEN: _____

WHOM: _____

HOW: _____

_____

_____

2. PERSONAL GROOMING

Take a good look at yourself right now. Are your hands and fingernails clean? Are your clothes clean and unwrinkled? Is your face clean, your hair neat?

Personal grooming—that is, personal neatness and cleanliness—is important in the work world. You are expected to be clean and neat when you are interviewing for a job, when you work in an office, and when you deal with the public. Even in jobs where the work gets you dirty, you are not supposed to show up already dirty at the start of the work day.

This unit will give you some idea of what kinds of clothing and personal grooming are expected in the job world.

PERSONAL GROOMING

Why Bother?

The impression you make on people will play a large part in determining whether you will be hired, keep your job, or even be promoted. This is why good grooming is so important. If you look sloppy, dirty, or careless, employers will presume that you will do your job tasks the same way.

Look at Jim, then answer the following questions.

1. If you walked in and saw Jim, would you do business with this travel agency? ☐ YES ☐ NO   Explain your answer. _____

2. What does his personal appearance tell you about Jim?

3. What does Jim's personal appearance tell you about the travel agency he works for?

4. Do you think you would get good service from Jim? ☐ YES   ☐ NO Explain your answer. _____

_____

_____

What to Wear?

The people below are getting ready to go to work. Decide what each should wear. Using the list, write in the items of clothing you recommend across from each person's name. It's OK to recommend the same item of clothing for different people. Add to the list if you wish.

cap	slacks	nylons
hat	jeans	socks
uniform	coveralls	work shoes
tie	dress	casual shoes
dress shirt	skirt	blouse
sport shirt	jewelry:	boots
scarf	(specify what you think would be all right to wear)	dress shoes

1. Maggie, a lawyer _____

2. Bill, a truckdriver for a
   gravel and stone company _____

3. Jackie, a salesperson in an
   auto parts store _____

4. Mike, a dental assistant _____

5. Frank, a salesperson in an
   exclusive clothing store.

_____

_____

_____

_____

6. Ann, a busdriver

_____

_____

_____

_____

Taking A Look At Yourself

Personal hygiene and cleanliness are necessary parts of good grooming. It is never appropriate to go to work sloppy or dirty. However, as you saw in the last activity, the particular clothes you wear will be determined by the type of job you have.

1. What is your present job? _____

   If you do not have a job, what job would you like to have? _____

2. What clothing is appropriate for your job or the job you would like to have? (Choose from the list in the last activity, or list items of your own choice.) _____

   _____

   _____

3. Check the items of your personal appearance that your boss in the job you listed above would want you to be careful about.

   _____ dirty fingernails   _____ dirty shirt

   _____ dirty hands   _____ dirty neck

   _____ unshaven face   _____ dirty ears

   _____ unshined, dirty shoes   _____ baggy pants

   _____ hair not combed   _____ bad breath

   _____ sloppy clothes   _____ missing buttons

   _____ dirty cuffs   _____ hair too long

   _____ dirty collar   _____ inappropriate dress

   _____ dirty hair   _____ inappropriate jewelry

   _____ dandruff   _____ other: _____

3. COOPERATION WITH THE EMPLOYER

Your boss is the person who employs you or who supervises your work. He or she keeps track of the work you are doing and how well you are doing it.

You do not just work *for* your employer. You have to work, cooperatively, *with* your employer as well. He or she cannot spend time checking on your every move, explaining the reasons behind every order, or arguing with you over company rules. For the relationship between you and your employer to be a good one, you have to work cooperatively.

This unit will introduce you to a few of the many kinds of situations in which cooperation with your employer is vital to your doing your job.

Pressures on the Boss

Cooperating with your employer or supervisor helps to keep the business running smoothly. Your boss has many responsibilities that you do not have. Often employees are not aware of the pressures that the boss may be under.

Some of the pressures and responsibilities that supervisors and bosses have are listed below. If you have a job, check those that apply to your supervisor or boss. If you do not have a job, interview someone who does. Find out which apply to his or her boss, and check them.

Every boss or supervisor has other duties in addition to those listed. In the spaces provided, add any that have been left out that apply to your boss or the boss of the person you interviewed.

_____ Must make sure that employees get their paychecks.

_____ Takes care of complaints from angry customers.

_____ When equipment breaks down, makes sure it gets repaired.

_____ Required to show that the business is making a profit.

_____ Keeps track of budgets for payroll, equipment, supplies, etc.

_____ Orders supplies or merchandise for the business.

_____ Makes sure there are enough employees to do the company's work.

_____ Arranges for security for the business.

_____ Settles disagreements between employees.

_____ Handles employee complaints.

Other: _____

_____

_____

_____

_____

_____

_____

Different Types of Bosses

There are many different kinds of bosses in the work world. Some are easier to get along with than others. Some of these different kinds of bosses are listed below.

Match each boss with his or her description:

A. Confused boss

B. Loud boss

C. Quiet boss

D. Perfectionist boss

E. Easy-going boss

F. Double boss

_F__ 1. Two bosses give you orders.

_D__ 2. This boss never seems satisfied with your work, and wants it done better.

_C__ 3. This boss doesn't talk much, so you may wonder if you're doing the job right.

_A__ 4. This boss may get upset and give orders that contradict each other and that you can't understand.

_B__ 5. Shouting or sounding rough are ways that this boss tells what he or she wants done.

_E__ 6. This boss doesn't make heavy demands on you. Be careful not to take advantage of this boss.

Accepting Orders

One way employees show cooperation is by the way they respond when the boss gives an order.

Three types of responses to requests or orders are described below. Add your own ideas on the blank lines.

1. **Defensive Employee**—resents orders

    May respond by:

    defending own actions

    pouting

    purposely carrying out orders very slowly

    threatening to quit

    folding arms

    feeling picked on

    _____

    _____

2. **Offensive Employee**—openly defiant of orders

    May respond by:

    arguing

    complaining

    yelling

    giving dirty looks

    refusing to carry out orders

    slamming doors

    _____

    _____

3. **Cooperative Employee**—accepts orders

    May respond by:

    smiling

    asking questions if there is a problem

    carrying out orders promptly

giving appropriate verbal response

raising reasonable objections privately and calmly

_____

_____

Responses to Situations

Here are some situations involving different bosses. For each situation, give an example of the three common responses. The first one is done for you. If you need ideas, look at the samples on the preceding page.

1. The office where you work is getting very busy. You are trying to finish your filing. The boss yells at you to type some memos.

   Possible responses are:

   DEFENSIVE: Type the memos very slowly so the boss will know that you don't like being yelled at.

   OFFENSIVE: Yell back at the boss loudly, "Make up your mind. What do you want, memos or filing?"

   COOPERATIVE: Say, "All right," and type the memos.

2. You work in a paint store, and you have just finished putting away some of the paint that was delivered today. Your boss says that you put some things in the wrong places.

   Possible responses are:

   DEFENSIVE: _____

   _____

   OFFENSIVE: _____

   _____

   COOPERATIVE: _____

   _____

3. Your boss is a Quiet Boss. She never says much to you. You wish she would tell you if you are doing a good job.

   Possible responses are:

   DEFENSIVE: _____

   _____

   OFFENSIVE: _____

   _____

   COOPERATIVE: _____

   _____

4. You work in a garden apartment building in a small town. Your boss sometimes confuses you. When you came to work you were told to sweep the hall. The boss sees you sweeping the hall and now asks you to mow the lawn right away.

Possible responses are:

DEFENSIVE: _____

_____

OFFENSIVE: _____

_____

COOPERATIVE: _____

_____

5. Your boss asks you to help a new employee.

Possible responses are:

DEFENSIVE: _____

_____

OFFENSIVE: _____

_____

COOPERATIVE: _____

_____

6. The store where you work has more than one boss. The manager tells you to finish the inventory. Another boss comes out and tells you to wait on the customers.

Possible responses are:

DEFENSIVE: _____

_____

OFFENSIVE: _____

_____

COOPERATIVE: _____

_____

7. Your boss tells you that you wrote up a sales slip the wrong way, then shows you how to do it correctly.

Possible responses are:

DEFENSIVE: _____

_____

OFFENSIVE: _____

_____

COOPERATIVE: _____

_____

Accepting Criticism

Some employees don't know how to accept criticism. They get hurt or angry feelings and don't understand that sometimes criticism is necessary. When is criticism necessary or helpful? What is the purpose of criticism? List your ideas below:

1. _____

2. _____

3. _____

4. _____

Below are six ways that people react to criticism. Match these reactions on the left with the ten responses on the right. (Reactions may be used more than once.)

A. Makes excuses

B. Argues

C. Puts responsibility on others

D. Pouts or sulks

E. Complains about being picked on

F. Compares self to others

___ 1. "If this office weren't so noisy, I could hear better. Then I'd be able to take complete phone messages."

___ 2. "What's wrong with this? I saw Joe do it this way."

___ 3. "How come I always get blamed for everything around here?"

___ 4. "I was so here on time. I know because I looked at the clock when I came in."

___ 5. "I told my mother to call in for me. She must have forgotten."

___ 6. Won't talk or smile for the rest of the day.

___ 7. "That's the way Rita showed me how to write the order. It's not my fault."

___ 8. "I think the computer messed the inventory up. You know how machines are."

___ 9. "I work just as fast as everybody else around here."

___ 10. "I was not on the phone for 15 minutes. Can you prove it?"

Chapter Review

Read the statements below. Decide if each is true or false, and write T or F on the line. Correct any statements that are false by writing a correct sentence below the false statement.

_F_ 1. The employer has many responsibilities that you don't see.

_____

_F_ 2. The employer who may get upset at times and gives orders that you can't understand, is called the double boss.

_____

_F_ 3. Some employees take advantage of bosses who are easy-going.

_____

_F_ 4. Criticism is a suggestion for improvement.

_____

_F_ 5. A good employee will respond negatively to criticism.

_____

Match the responses in Column A with the items in Column B. Terms in Column A may be used more than once.

COLUMN A

A. Defensive

B. Offensive

C. Cooperative

COLUMN B

_B_ 1. Openly defiant of orders.

_A_ 2. Defends own actions.

_B_ 3. Refuses to carry out orders.

_C_ 4. Accepts orders.

_A_ 5. Resents orders.

_A_ 6. Complains

_C_ 7. Raises reasonable objections privately.

Name four ways that people react to criticism and give an example of each.

Reaction	Example
1. _____	_____
2. _____	_____
3. _____	_____
4. _____	_____

29

4. COOPERATION WITH CO-WORKERS

On most jobs, you don't work alone. You work with other people.

When you start work, everybody else on the job will have been on the job longer than you. They all know more about how things are done than you do.

But they're all just people, like yourself. They have the same kinds of needs and wants that you do. You'll like some of them a lot, others less so. But in all cases, you are expected to get along with your co-workers and to cooperate with them in getting the job done.

This unit will help you explore some of the problems you might encounter in cooperating with your co-workers, and will suggest ways of successfully overcoming these problems.

You have been assigned a special project by your employer, Mrs. Fargate. She has asked that you choose three of your co-workers to work with you as a team. Below are descriptions of eight of your co-workers. They are all good workers, but each has a different style of working with others. Decide which three you would want on your team by checking the box after each description. Give a reason for each choice.

Gary   Seems very friendly at first. However, he has a way of getting you to talk about yourself and then tells everyone else what you've said when you're not around. He also tells you things about other co-workers. Sometimes you secretly enjoy hearing about who's dating whom or whom the boss yelled at, but other times you think that Gary goes too far.

_____ Yes _____ No   Why or why not? _____

_____

Shawn   Talks mostly about herself. If she's not talking about her great boyfriend or new car, she's telling you how she "told the boss off."

_____ Yes _____ No   Why or why not? _____

_____

Brett   Always seems to act like he's something he's not. When the boss called him into her office to talk to him about a problem he was having, he told everyone that the boss just wanted to thank him for doing a good job. Several times he's made up stories about customers complimenting him.

_____ Yes _____ No   Why or why not? _____

_____

Gene   Likes to tell everyone else what to do. He's a hard worker and although he has a good knowledge of what needs to be done, he tends to order other workers around.

_____ Yes _____ No   Why or why not? _____

_____

Polly   Has a tendency to find something wrong with everyone. She is a perfectionist and expects everyone else to be perfect, too. She'll be glad to tell you how you could have done a better job, and you don't even have to ask her!

_____ Yes _____ No   Why or why not? _____

_____

Sandy

Is a talented person, but tries to outdo her co-workers. Her main concern is whether she can do a better job than everyone else.

_____ Yes _____ No   Why or why not? _____

_____

Pat

Usually has a smile and nice word for everyone. Pat helps co-workers if they get behind in their work and listens to their problems.

_____ Yes _____ No   Why or why not? _____

_____

Joshua

Interrupts others constantly. He breaks into conversations to give his opinion, tell a joke, or slap someone on the back.

_____ Yes _____ No   Why or why not? _____

_____

Identifying Behaviors

In the last exercise you decided which people you did or did not want to work with on an assignment. By doing that, you made some judgments about the type of people you dislike working with. But since you don't know these people personally, what you're saying is that you dislike their *behavior*, not the people themselves. They may have some very nice qualities, too. If you can identify the behaviors that annoy you, you can concentrate on dealing with these behaviors rather than disliking the whole person.

Using the descriptions given in the last exercise, match the behavior in Column A with the person in Column B.

Column A	**Column B**
_____1. competitive	A. Gary
_____2. lying	B. Shawn
_____3. friendly	C. Brett
_____4. bragging	D. Gene
_____5. aggressive	E. Polly
_____6. gossiping	F. Sandy
_____7. bossy	G. Pat
_____8. critical	H. Joshua

Understanding Unpleasant Behavior

Most everyone has worked with persons who are unpleasant at times. But many people do not know how to deal with the kinds of people described in the last two exercises. The next few pages will discuss some solutions to this problem.

If you try to understand how these persons think and feel, it may help you in working with them.

For example, why do you think Gary gossips so much? Perhaps he doesn't feel so good about himself and thinks that talking about other people will make him important. Although you still may not approve of his gossiping, understanding *why* he does this may cause you to dislike him less.

Look at the other people we've mentioned, and give a possible reason for each of their behaviors:

1. Why does Shawn brag so much? _____

_____

_____

2. Why does Brett try to cover up his failures? _____

_____

_____

3. Why is Gene so bossy? _____

_____

_____

4. Why is Polly so critical? _____

_____

_____

5. Why is Sandy so competitive? _____

_____

_____

6. Why does Joshua interrupt constantly? _____

_____

_____

Understanding Your Feelings/ Attitudes

Think about how you feel toward people you dislike at work or at school. Ask yourself these questions:

	Yes	No
A. Are you able to separate the behavior from the person?	_____	_____
B. Do you try to understand why a person might behave in a certain way?	_____	_____
C. Do you look for the positive qualities in a person, to balance the things you don't like about him/her?	_____	_____
D. Are you aware of how your own attitude/feelings may be affecting your behavior towards others?	_____	_____

Since you can't change other people, you may have to change your attitude in order to get along with others. If you answered "no" to any of the above questions, then you need to think about changing your attitude towards your co-workers. Everyone has a choice: to react *positively* or *negatively* to other people.

In this section you will see how two different personalities (positive and negative) respond to the same situation. Below each response, circle whether the thought is positive or negative. The first one is done for you.

1. You've decided to try and lose some weight, but everyone where you work is always snacking. When you turned down the donuts that were passed around this morning, one of your co-workers said, "I bet you don't last a week on this diet!"

I think I'll tell him that he could stand to lose that spare tire around his waist. He's probably just jealous.

POSITIVE PERSONALITY

NEGATIVE PERSONALITY

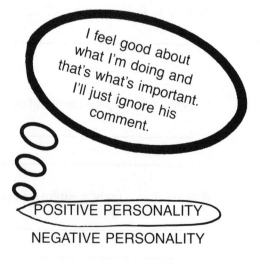

I feel good about what I'm doing and that's what's important. I'll just ignore his comment.

POSITIVE PERSONALITY

NEGATIVE PERSONALITY

2. You have just started writing the orders for your department. Because you are still learning, you mistakenly ordered too much merchandise. A co-worker looks at the extra items and says to you, "Were you drunk when you wrote that order, or what?"

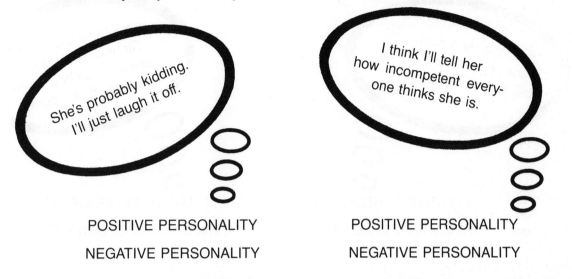

POSITIVE PERSONALITY

NEGATIVE PERSONALITY

POSITIVE PERSONALITY

NEGATIVE PERSONALITY

3. Jake comes over to your work station and says, "I heard Henry asking Sue to go out with him. She turned him down. What a laugh!"

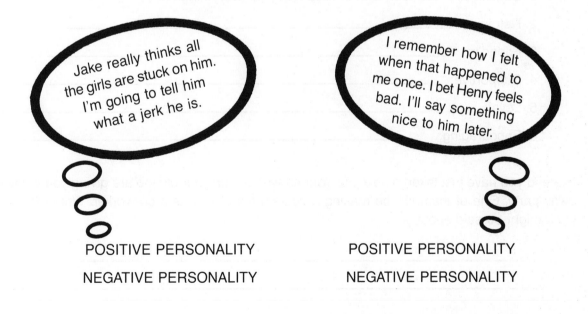

POSITIVE PERSONALITY

NEGATIVE PERSONALITY

POSITIVE PERSONALITY

NEGATIVE PERSONALITY

4. It's really a busy day at work. You're working as fast as you can. Stephanie, a co-worker, comes by and tells you to hurry up.

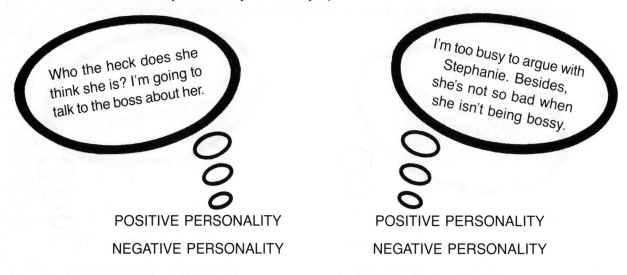

POSITIVE PERSONALITY

NEGATIVE PERSONALITY

POSITIVE PERSONALITY

NEGATIVE PERSONALITY

Listed below are six qualities—six positive ways of interacting with co-workers. Give an example of something you could say that shows each quality. The first one is done for you.

1. Sensitive: "You look kind of tired today. Is everything okay?"

2. Helpful: "_____"

3. Friendly: "_____"

4. Supportive: "_____"

5. Loyal: "_____"

6. Encouraging: "_____"

Pretend you have just taken a new job. Your co-workers on your old job are giving you a going-away party. One of them will be making a speech about you as a co-worker. Write what you think might be said about you:

5. THE TELEPHONE

Next to face-to-face conversation, the most important communications tool in the business world is the telephone. Most businesses could not operate at all without it.

As an employee, you will probably have to communicate with others on the telephone, both in your own organization and outside it. You should become thoroughly familiar with the courtesy customs of making or receiving a business telephone call. A business call is quite different from the friendly calls you make on your home phone, and it is handled differently.

This unit will show you some of the differences, and will teach you how to handle routine business telephone calls courteously and efficiently.

Using the Telephone Effectively

The phone is an important tool in the world of work. Imagine what would happen to our businesses if the phone system stopped working for just a single day. Many important calls would not be made, and companies could lose millions of dollars.

You have an important part to play at work when you use your company's phone. When you do, the first thing to keep in mind is: develop a good personal telephone style. Since the person to whom you are talking can't see you, you have to rely on your voice to show you are interested.

Here are some ways you can show interest on the phone:

1. Speak clearly. Don't mumble words.

2. Speak neither too loud nor too soft.

3. Speak neither too fast nor too slow.

4. Try to picture the person at the other end of the line. Talk *to* the person, not *at* the phone. You can do that by raising and lowering your voice so you do not speak in only one tone.

Practice developing your personal telephone style. Take turns reading the telephone message below. While each person is reading, use the checklist to grade the readers in their personal telephone style: A (very good), B (fair), C (poor).

"Good morning, Mrs. Jones. This is Joe Rafel from Mason's T.V. Repair. I am calling to tell you that your T.V. set is now ready to be picked up. We are open from 9 a.m. to 5 p.m. daily. However, we are closed during the lunch hours. Your bill for the repair is the amount we told you two days ago: $35.64."

Put rating **grades** under columns at the right for:	Clear and Distinct	Volume (Loud/Soft)	Rate (Fast/Slow)
1st READER			
2nd READER			
3rd READER			
4th READER			

The following rules for telephone courtesy are simple. Use these rules to make a good impression on the phone caller.

---

1. Answer the phone right away. Try to answer after the first ring.

2. Give your name and place of business.
   Say: "Hello, this is Merchandise Company, Randy Martinez speaking. Can I help you?"
   Not: "Hi, Randy here."

3. Talk in a businesslike way, not in a casual style.
   Say: "Excuse me, may I take your name and number?"
   Not: "Huh, what's your name and number?"

4. Use the words "May" or "Please" when you need information.
   Say: "May I have your name and your company's name?"
   Not: "Give me your name and company and I'll have Joe call you."

5. Use the caller's name occasionally. It's nice to be called by your name, especially on the phone.

Put a line through the statements below that are not courteous or businesslike. Write a courteous, businesslike message next to each statement you have crossed out.

	Statement	**Your Response**
1.	"Listen, sweetheart. You gotta speak louder if you want me to hear you."	_____
2.	"Yes, Mrs. Bashad, I'll tell my manager you called."	_____
3.	"Hi, who's calling?"	_____
4.	"Give me your name and I'll have him give you a buzz."	_____
5.	"May I have your name and number so I can tell Mrs. Parsons you called?"	_____

6. "O.K., O.K., I got the message." _____

7. "He's tied up right now. I'll have him call you back." _____

Giving Information:

You should be careful when giving information to a caller. It may be embarrassing if you say where your employer or another worker is. It would not be businesslike to say:

"Miss Jones is in the washroom right now."

A better way would be:

"Miss Jones is not at her desk right now. But I will give her your message."

In the activity below, circle which messages would be better to give a caller. In the space provided write why you chose each message.

1. "Mr. Washington is out of the city." **Or** "Mr. Washington is in New York to discuss a contract."

_____

2. "When Miss Lopez returns to her desk, I'll give her your message." **Or** "Miss Lopez had to go up to see the boss. She should be returning to her desk in about 15 minutes."

_____

3. "Mrs. De Carlo, our manager, is somewhere at the Linton Hotel on business. Maybe you can reach her there." **Or** "Mrs. De Carlo, our manager, will be in tomorrow morning. May I ask her to call you?"

_____

4. "Mr. Tomson is out of the office right now. Would you like to leave a message?" **Or** "I don't know where the dickens Mr. Tomson is. He was here about a minute ago. Just a minute, I'll have to go look for him."

_____

5. "Ms. Richards will be in the office tomorrow morning. May I ask her to call you then?" **Or** "Ms. Richards had to go see a guy from IBM. When she gets back, I'll ask her to call you."

_____

Sometimes you have to get important information from a caller. For example, suppose you work for a company that mails products across the nation. If you are taking orders, it is important that you listen carefully and write down the following information:

1. What was ordered
2. Where it should be mailed
3. To whom it should be mailed
4. Who should receive the bill

Marlo works at Mile High Pizza. She is taking a pizza order on the phone from Randy Martinez. Randy wants the pizza to be delivered to his apartment. Write in the space below the information Marlo should ask Randy.

_____

_____

_____

_____

_____

Miss Jameson calls you at Allparts Tire Company. She wants to order some tires for her car. What information should you get from Miss Jameson?

_____

_____

_____

_____

_____

You should end a conversation in a friendly, but businesslike manner. Let the caller hang up first to show you are not in a hurry. Before you hang up, thank the person with a comment such as:

"Thank you for calling, Miss Jackson."
Or
"Thank you for the information. I'll be sure to give it to Mr. DeCoza."

Problem Callers:
You may occasionally have to talk to a caller who is angry. You should never respond in anger. Instead, remain calm and try to solve the problem. If you can't, politely ask the caller to wait while you contact your manager.

Match the statement in Column B that offers the best response to each of the angry messages in Column A. (Some responses in Column B should be left blank—they're bad responses.)

Column A	**Column B**
A. "I bought a tape recorder from you just two days ago, and already it's broken! What kind of junk are you people selling, anyway?"	_____ 1. "Get off my back, will ya? I just work here."
B. "I put my order in three weeks ago and it's not in yet! Don't you believe in taking care of your customers?"	_____ 2. "I'm sorry you haven't received your order. If you'll give me the order number, I'll be glad to check it out."
C. "I know your voice! I spoke to you before about your lousy service. I don't want to talk to you. Isn't there anyone there who can get things straight?"	_____ 3. "Listen, nobody's perfect. We're doing the best we can."
	_____ 4. "At this point, maybe you should talk to my manager. I'll be glad to get her for you."
	_____ 5. "We don't sell junk, lady. We sell quality merchandise."
	_____ 6. "I'm sorry to hear you're having trouble. Please hold and I'll put you in touch with our Repair Department."

Taking Messages

One of the most important tasks you may have is to take messages. The message should be written down on paper. Most companies have a form like the one below. Write the information down while you're talking to the caller. Don't wait until later or you might forget something. The message should be written or printed clearly and it should include:

1. The date and exact time of the call.

2. The name of the caller and company (check to make sure you spell names correctly).

3. The telephone number, including extension and the area code if it is a long distance call.

4. The details of the message.

5. The initials of the person who wrote the message.

YOU
WERE
OUT

For *Miss Capodice*

Date *1/8/86*　　　Time *10:30 am*

M rs. *Michaeleen*

of *Community Hospital*

312-697-5555 She has

information you wanted

☑ Please return call by *2 pm today*

☐ Will phone again _____

In the form below, look at the information Ed O'Brien wrote down, after talking with Miss Rowell. Write on the message form any information Ed did not include.

Ed O'Brien:　"Chase Sanson Company, Ed O'Brien speaking. May I help you?"

Miss Rowell:　"This is Miss Rowell of 2nd City Bank. Please tell Ron Garcia that I'll be meeting him for lunch on Thursday, at 11:30 at Michael's Restaurant. Ask him to bring copies of the office plans."

YOU WERE OUT

For _RON_
Date _THURS._ Time _____
M _ROWELL_
of _____
WILL MEET YOU FOR
LUNCH

☐ Please return call by _____
☐ Will phone again _____

The following telephone calls were received on March 5. Take the messages on the forms provided below.

William McEnroe of Chicago called Mr. Alfred Rogers at 10:00 a.m. regarding Order C-1350. Mr. McEnroe's telephone number is (312) 888-3695. He'll call again at 2:30 p.m.

YOU WERE OUT

For _____
Date _____ Time _____
M _____
of _____
_____
_____

☐ Please return call by _____
☐ Will phone again _____

Mrs. Sandy Phillips of Philadelphia called Mr. Jose Giraldo at 1:45 p.m. She said she received Order Number 1026, but not order Number 1027. Her telephone number is (215) 679-5321. She wants Mr. Giraldo to call her back today.

YOU WERE OUT

For _____

Date _____ Time _____

M _____

of _____

_____

_____

☐ **Please return call by** _____

☐ **Will phone again** _____

A Note About Personal Telephone Calls

The policy on using the business phone for personal calls depends on the company where you work. Most companies do not allow this. Personal calls should be made only when absolutely necessary. You should ask permission from your employer, and the call should be brief. If you receive a personal call at work, end the conversation quickly.

Chapter Review

A. PERSONAL TELEPHONE STYLE

Add at least two ways to improve your telephone style and to show personal interest on the phone:

1. Speak clearly

2. _____

3. _____

B. TELEPHONE COURTESY. Add at least two rules of courtesy to the ones listed for making a good impression on the phone.

1. Talk in a business-like way.

2. Use the caller's name occasionally.

3. _____

4. _____

C. HANDLING INCOMING CALLS AND PERSONAL TELEPHONE CALLS. Based on the information you read in this chapter, match items listed in Column B with those in Column A. Some items in Column B may be used twice. Some may not be used at all.

Column A	**Column B**
____1. Completing the call	a. End the conversation quickly.
____2. Problem callers	b. Do not always tell where the employer is.
____3. Giving information	c. Thank the caller for phoning.
____4. Personal telephone calls	d. You may have to contact the manager.
____5. Taking an order on the phone	e. Listen carefully and write down the message.
	f. Never speak in anger.
	g. Write down the initials of the person who took the message.
	h. Do this seldom.

D. TAKING MESSAGES. Write up the following message on the form below.

At 9:15 a.m., Mrs. Carla Santoya of the Santoya Sisters Manufacturing Company called your employer. Mrs. Santoya wants to be called back today. She can be reached at 405-321-4670, until 2:00 p.m. After that, she can be reached at 405-654-5777 until 5 p.m. She said to tell your employer she needs to order more materials.

YOU
WERE
OUT

For _____

Date _____ Time _____

M _____

of _____

_____

_____

☐ **Please return call by** _____

☐ **Will phone again** _____

6. THE PUBLIC

If you work for a business, everybody who is not employed by that business is a member of the public.

You may work for a business, but your business works for its customers. And its customers are part of the public. So whether you think of it or not, you are really working for members of the public.

The public is vital to your business. It's vital to your job. It's part of your job to learn how to deal politely and efficiently with the public, even when it's hard to do so.

This unit will show you what is expected of you on the job in your dealings with the public. It will also give you some tips on how to handle some of the trouble situations that can arise in dealing with the public.

1. Who is the Public?

In this chapter, the public is any person who receives a service in a place such as a business, a government agency, or an office. That service you receive could include buying clothes in a department store, mailing a package at the local post office, or borrowing a book from the public library. You receive many of these services every day. You, your friends, and your family *are* the public.

Have you been to any of the places below? If you have, you have been a member of the public. Check those places you visited in the past two weeks.

___drug store	___clothing store	___movie theatre
___library	___post office	___restaurant
___bank	___record store	___games room
___doctor's office	___unemployment office	___grocery store

2. Why Treat the Public Well?

When you receive a service, you want to be treated courteously. So do other people. They expect to be treated well when they come to your place of work for a service.

The public is vital to your job. If you treat customers well, you will feel better. They will feel better. The place where you work will be a better, friendlier place to work.

There are many other reasons for treating people courteously when they come to your place of work. Think of 3, and write them down.

1. _____

_____

2. _____

_____

3. _____

_____

3. **What Kind of Bad Service Really Bugs You?**

Look over the list of annoying situations below. Add other items that have bothered you. Finally, rank order, from 1 to 10, the situations that most upset you.

_____standing a long time in a line waiting to be served

_____being ignored, or half-listened to

_____being short-changed

_____having to wait at a doctor's office

_____not finding something you wanted because the store ran out of the item

_____an employee spending too much time with one customer while you're waiting to be served

_____taking an item home, and finding something wrong with it

_____being kept on "hold" when you phone a place of business

_____not being given a sincere "thank you" when you pay for a service

_____a clerk not keeping a promise made to you (like being promised an item on Thursday, and finding it won't come until Saturday)

_____not having someone return a phone call after you left a message

_____placing a catalogue order and receiving the wrong items

_____ordering a hot meal and having it served to you cold

_____being repeatedly approached by a sales person (or clerk) in a store trying to sell you something

_____ _____

_____ _____

_____ _____

_____ _____

_____ _____

De-bugging Bad Service

On the previous page, you ranked items that irritated you. On this page, choose the items you ranked in the top 6. Then write how you would act to help solve the problem if you were the employee in that situation.

If you chose "standing in a line waiting to be served," you might handle the situation by saying to waiting people:

> "I'm sorry you have to wait this long. We are moving as fast as we can to make sure you are served soon."

Or you might try to speed things up. Or you might see if you could get another employee to help wait on some of the customers.

TOPIC ITEMS	HOW YOU WOULD ACT
1. _____	_____
	_____
	_____
2. _____	_____
	_____
	_____
3. _____	_____
	_____
	_____
4. _____	_____
	_____
	_____
5. _____	_____
	_____
	_____
6. _____	_____
	_____
	_____

Rules for Dealing with the Public

Below is a list of rules to follow when dealing with the public.

    A. Be pleasant and smile.

    B. If possible, use the name of the person.

    C. Show you have a sincere interest in the customer's needs.

    D. Provide prompt and courteous service.

    E. Apologize to people who have to wait a long time.

    F. Answer the customer's questions.

    G. Be patient and listen.

    H. Answer the phone promptly.

    I. Help customers if you can; find someone else to help them if you can't.

    J. Show you appreciate the public's business or interest by saying, "Thank you."

    K. Don't make promises if you can't keep them.

    L. Don't argue with the public.

1. Martha is a clerk at City Hall. A couple arrives to request a marriage license. Martha is in a hurry to get to lunch. She ignores several questions the couple asks her. She makes out the license and gives it to them without saying anything.

    Which rules did Martha not put into practice? (Write the letters in front of the rules.)

    _____

    What would you have said or done to treat this couple more courteously?

    _____

    _____

2. Winfield is Assistant Manager at High Value Food Store. A child accidentally broke a bottle of apple sauce. The father apologized to Winfield. Winfield looked disgusted and yelled at one of his workers to "clean up the mess."

    Which rules did Winfield not put into practice?_____

    _____

    What would you have said or done to treat the person more courteously?_____

    _____

    _____

    _____

3. Terri is a receptionist at Community Rehabilitation Center. One of the parents who visits the Center often, Mrs. Brown, walked in and demanded to see the supervisor. She complained about how poorly the Center was treating her child. Terri started to explain to her that the Center does not have enough workers. The woman continued to argue, and Terri, trying to be loyal, continued to defend the Center.

Which rules did Terri not put into practice?_____

What would you have said or done to treat the person more courteously?_____

_____

_____

_____

4. About 200 people have been standing in line for 4 hours to purchase tickets to a rock concert at Oak Stream Concert Center. Vitas, the manager, is nervous about the people having to wait so long in line. He puts pressure on the ticket vendors to sell tickets faster, but they are already going as fast as they can.

Which rules did Vitas not put into practice?_____

What would you have said or done to treat the persons in line more courteously?_____

_____

_____

_____

Dealing with the Angry Member of the Public

Here are some rules and examples to follow when dealing with an angry member of the Public.

What you should do if a person is angry	Example
1. Listen carefully to the angry person.	Look at the eyes of the other person, nod your head, use facial expressions.
2. Don't take the anger personally, even if the angry person blames you personally.	Say to yourself: "This person is not angry at me. The poor service has upset him."
3. Say something to the person to show you understand his or her anger.	"I understand that you're very upset ..."
4. Indicate some action you will take, or you will ask your supervisor to take.	"I will see my supervisor right now and ask her to help you."

Indicate whether the following statements about dealing with an angry person are True or False by writing T or F in front of each. Be prepared to discuss your answers.

1. ___ The first thing to do with an angry person is to listen.
2. ___ Arguing with people is the best thing to do because it shows you take them seriously.
3. ___ It is better to say nothing to people after they show anger. Otherwise, you could make them more angry by what you say.
4. ___ It is always a good idea to tell angry people you will take some action to handle the problem that's making them angry.
5. ___ To reduce the person's anger, tell him/her that you will act on the problem immediately.
6. ___ If people are waiting in line for a long time, try not to look at them because they might yell at you. It's not your fault, anyway.
7. ___ Even if the problem is not your fault, you should say you are sorry that it happened.

People Who May Need Extra Help

Some members of the public may need extra help. They are:

- Elderly people

- Parents with babies

- People who can't speak English

- Disabled persons, like:

    —those on crutches
    —blind people
    —those in wheelchairs
    —the hard of hearing

Most of the time, these customers want to do things for themselves. The best help you can give is to respect the customer's independence. If you think a customer needs extra help, *ask first*: "May I help you?"

Here are ideas to keep in mind for each of these customers:

1. Helping an older customer: Some older people may need extra help. They may not be physically strong, or they may have poor hearing or eyesight. Not all older people have these problems. You have to pay attention to see if they need your help.

2. Helping customers with babies: Fathers or mothers with small babies may need extra help. They have their hands full. To help them, you can: open a door, carry a package, or get something that's out of reach.

3. People who don't speak English as their native language: Give extra time to these customers. Be patient and do your best to figure out what they are saying. Speak clearly and smile. Point to what you are talking about if that will help. Speak slowly. Don't use slang.

4. Customers on crutches: A customer on crutches may need help getting through a door or finding a place to sit in a crowded restaurant. The person who puts crutches aside to sit down will still want to have them close by. Never take them away unless the person requests it.

5. Blind people: Blind customers do not want to be treated as if they were helpless. Ask how you can help, and explain to them what you are doing. Blind people will probably tell you how you can help.

6. People in wheelchairs: These people sometimes cannot reach things, open doors, etc. Offer to help before actually doing anything. This shows them you respect their independence.

7. Customers with poor hearing: If a customer seems to have trouble hearing, try to look at the person when you talk. Even people who can't read lips will understand and feel better if they can see your face. Don't yell or talk extra slow. A smile always helps.

Chapter Review

1. Write three reasons why you should treat the public well:

   a. _____

   b. _____

   c. _____

2. Put a line through the item, or items below that were *not* listed as rules for dealing with the public:

   a. if possible, use the name of the person
   b. answer the customer's questions
   c. stay near the customer while he/she is looking at items in the store
   d. answer the phone promptly
   e. provide prompt and courteous service
   f. be friendly by talking to a customer as long as they would like to talk, even though other customers are waiting

3. MATCHING. Match the statements in Column B that best fit the statement in Column A.

Column A	Column B
_____ a. taking an item home and finding something wrong with it	1. reason for treating the public well
_____ b. the public is your job	2. one rule for dealing with the public
_____ c. customer with poor hearing	3. place where you are a member of the public
_____ d. answer the phone promptly	4. something that may "bug" you as a member of the public
_____ e. older people	5. one thing you should do if a person is angry
_____ f. indicate some action you will take	6. may need extra help because they may not be physically strong
_____ g. post office	7. especially for this person, try to look at the person when you talk

4. You are the assistant manager of the Golden Globe Movie Theater. The people have lined up for popcorn and pop at the counter. However, there is no order to who goes first and some customers are beginning to complain about not being served in order. Others are "butting in" or shouting out their order so they can be served first, even though they lined up after those in front of them.

What would you do? _____

_____

_____

_____

_____

7. COMMUNICATION

Throughout this book you will see the importance of communication on the job. In order to cooperate with co-workers, you must listen to them as well as make sure that you are clearly understood. This is also true when you are serving the public or cooperating with your employer. Many of the problems that occur on the job are the result of poor communication.

Barriers to Communication

An awareness of some of the barriers to communication can help you learn to communicate more effectively. Match each situation below to the communication barrier it describes.

A. During break time some of the employees were discussing rock groups. Marva had a different opinion from Jack. "You are wrong, and you're stupid," she told him, and walked out of the room.

A 1. criticizing instead of explaining

B. Barry never waits until a person has finished talking. He just breaks right into the conversation with his ideas.

E 2. poor eye contact

C. Jeremy was telling Sam about his experience with an angry customer. Even though Sam wasn't listening, he looked at Jeremy, nodded his head and said, "Uh-huh, uh-huh." When Jeremy finished talking, he asked, "What would you have told her?" Sam just looked at Jeremy and didn't know what to say.

3. ordering when you should be asking politely

D. Mr. Lee is putting all the jeans in his store on sale for $10.00. He wants Marissa to change the price tags. "Tag all the jeans at ten," he tells her. Marissa thinks she understands, and at exactly ten o'clock, she goes to put price tags on the jeans. She notices that they are already marked $13.99, and wonders why Mr. Lee told her to put price tags on them.

B 4. interrupting

E. Fred is telling Jane about the new company policy on borrowing equipment. Although she is listening, Jane keeps looking past Fred at the doorway, so she can see when her boyfriend comes in.

C 5. thinking ahead when you should be listening

F. Brenda and Suzanne have not been getting along at work. Brenda approaches Suzanne and says, I really think we should talk about our differences." Suzanne turns to Carl, another worker, and says, "Are you going to the game this weekend?"

6. fear of speaking up

G. Dave is a new employee. He has been asked to handle the mail. He goes to Diane to ask her a question about how to use the mailing machine. Diane says, "How many times do I have to explain this to you? Why don't you use your head once in a while?"

D 7. misunderstanding

H. Ellen was telling Gene about her new idea for a sales campaign. While she was talking, Gene kept thinking, "Wait until she hears my idea. I'll tell her all about the promotional possibilities. ..."

8. pretending to listen

I. Frank started working at the hospital one week ago. Mrs. Juarez, the supervisor, has been watching everything he does. This makes Frank very nervous, but he doesn't know how to tell her.

9. ignoring what is said

J. Mark turned from his cash register and said, "Jean, get me some quarters. I need them right away."

10. rudely disagreeing

Listening

One of the most important parts of communication is listening. Poor listening habits are usually the cause of communication problems. Rate your listening habits on the scale below by circling one of the numbers (1-5) after each item.

	USUALLY	OFTEN	SOMETIMES	NOT USUALLY	HARDLY EVER
1. After only a short period of listening, I start thinking about what I'm going to say next.	1	(2)	3	4	5
2. If I don't like the person, I don't really listen to what she/he is saying.	1	(2)	3	4	5
3. I interrupt others before they are finished talking.	1	(2)	3	4	5
4. I fake attention.	1	(2)	3	4	(5)
5. I talk mostly about myself.	1	2	3	4	(5)
6. I ask questions.	5	4	3	(2)	1
7. I give other people a chance to talk.	(5)	4	3	2	1
8. I try to see things from the other person's point of view.	5	(4)	3	2	1
9. I maintain good eye contact when listening.	5	(4)	3	2	1
10. I get so busy taking notes, that I miss some of what is said.	1	2	3	(4)	5
11. I get distracted easily.	(1)	2	3	4	5
12. I let my mind wander or I daydream when someone is talking.	(1)	2	3	4	5

ADD THE CIRCLED NUMBERS TO GET YOUR SCORE:_____

45-60 You are a good listener, and probably make few mistakes at work. More than likely, people enjoy talking to you and being with you.

(31-44) You need to improve your listening skills. This will also improve your job performance.

12-30 You are a poor listener. You have probably lost some friends or made mistakes at work because of your poor listening habits.

Paraphrasing

One way to improve communication is by *paraphrasing*. Paraphrasing means repeating what a person has said to you, but using slightly different words. This helps you to know whether you understood the message as it was intended.

Paraphrasing might begin something like this:

"If I understand you correctly . . . ."

"I hear you saying . . . . Is that correct?"

Show how paraphrasing can work in the following conversations. The first one is done for you.

A. We ran out of sale items this week. I'd like you to take care of that.

Are you saying that I should order more sales items for next week?

B. I want to go to the game next Saturday, but I'm afraid to ask for the day off.

You sound like you feel anxious about _____ _____

C. The new policy on cashing paychecks is really unfair.

Using "I" Messages

Using "I" messages is a skill that can be used when giving criticism, explaining a problem, making a suggestion, or expressing an opinion. The most important thing about "I" messages is that they don't make the other person feel offended by what you say. It doesn't blame "YOU"—the other person.

There are two parts to the "I" message. THE *FIRST PART* OF THE "I" MESSAGE describes your feelings *without blaming* anyone else for the way you feel:

"YOU" Message (blames others)	**"I" Message (first part)**
1. You really make me mad.	1. I'm feeling upset about this.
2. You sure are disorganized.	2. I like to have things well organized.
3. You're always interrupting.	3. Maybe I'm talking too much.
4. You don't understand.	4. _____
5. You're walking too fast.	5. _____
6. You're confusing me.	6. _____
7. Your smoking bothers me.	7. _____

Are you getting the idea? The first part of the "I" message describes your feelings. THE *SECOND PART* OF THE "I" MESSAGE describes how you would like to feel or how you would like the situation to be changed.

"I" Message—first part (describes your feelings)	**"I" Message—2nd part** (describes how you'd like things to change)
1. I'm having some difficulty following you.	1. Could we go back to the first part of your story?
2. Although I don't agree, I hear your point of view.	2. I'd like us to understand each other better.
3. I'm concerned about the image of our department.	3. I'm asking everyone to give special attention to personal appearance.

In the situations below, change the "YOU" Messages to "I" Messages. Use *both parts* of the "I" Message. The first one is done for you.

1. The night crew where you work is having a meeting to decide on a better system for ordering merchandise. Gary insists that he knows the best way and won't give anyone else a chance to talk.

"YOU" Message	"I" Message (1st part)	"I" Message (2nd part)
Gary, you're monopolizing the conversation.	Gary, I appreciate your good ideas.	I'd also like to hear some other opinions.

2. You're out to lunch with some of your co-workers. In a joking mood, they start to tease you about being the favorite of the boss. If your co-workers have a real problem over this, you would like to discuss it.

"YOU" Message	"I" Message (1st part)	"I" Message (2nd part)
If you worked as hard as I do, you might get noticed, too.		

3. You've just started a new job. The supervisor keeps watching everything you do. You would like to be able to work more on your own.

"YOU" Message	"I" Message (1st part)	"I" Message (2nd part)
You're making me nervous.		

4. Yvonne collects the money for the coffee fund at work. Everyone is supposed to contribute, and you're the only one who doesn't drink coffee.

"YOU" Message	"I" Message (1st part)	"I" Message (2nd part)
Yvonne, you're being unfair. You're the ones who drink the coffee.		

5. You've noticed the long checkout lines at work. You think that opening another express lane will help solve this problem. Mrs. Reed, your boss, walks by and you stop to tell her about it.

"YOU" Message	"I" Message (1st part)	"I" Message (2nd part)
Mrs. Reed, you really need to do something about these long lines.		

68

Chapter Review

1. List five barriers to communication.

   a. _____   b. _____   c. _____

   d. _____   e. _____

2. Check the items that show poor listening habits:

   _____ Interrupting

   _____ Asking questions

   _____ Pretending to listen

   _____ Good eye contact

   _____ Thinking ahead

   _____ Daydreaming

   _____ Letting others talk

3. Show how *paraphrasing* might work in this situation.
   Co-worker: "These printouts from the computer are all crazy. They're a waste of time."

   You: _____

   _____

4. Write an example of an "I" message to show how you can:

   a. express positive feelings (you like a change that was made on the job)

      _____

      _____

   b. stand up for your rights (you feel you were treated unfairly about something)

      _____

      _____

   c. express personal opinion, including disagreement (about the way some task should be done)

      _____

      _____

d. make requests, ask for help (about some supplies you have run out of)

_____

_____

e. express negative feelings (you are upset about something that happened)

_____

_____

f. refuse requests (because you're too busy to help right now)

_____

_____

8. DECISION MAKING

Your life in the world of work will be affected by the decisions you make. Some decisions are very basic. Whether or not you decide to show up for work, goof off on the job, steal from your employer, or gossip about co-workers can make the difference between whether you are a valued employee or someone who gets fired.

Other decisions require individual planning. Where you live, how you get to work, how to deal with a personal problem on the job—all can require careful thought. It is important for you to know how to make decisions that will help you on the job. The activities in this section will help show you how to make carefully planned decisions.

How Much Time Do You Spend on Decisions?

We make decisions every day. Some decisions are so routine that we hardly think about them. Other decisions are more important, so we might take a long time thinking about them.

Below is a list of decisions that you probably have faced or will face during your lifetime. Rank them according to the amount of time you expect to spend on each, using this code:

1. Routine; I wouldn't spend much time thinking about this before doing it (or not doing it).
2. I'd give this decision an average amount of time and thought.
3. I'd think about this carefully. I would take plenty of time making this decision.

Decision	Ranking
To go to work	1
To gossip about someone	1
What to eat	1
To get married	3
What time to get up in the morning	1
To smoke	1
To tell someone you're angry about something	3
To change jobs	3
What kind of car to buy	3
To ask someone for a date	3
What to spend your money on	2
What clothes to wear	2
What to do after high school	3
Which movie to see	2
To go to school	1
Which school to go to after high school	3

If you look back at how you ranked your decisions, you'll probably notice that some very important decisions are surprisingly easy to make and don't take much time at all. The decision to go to work, for example, is certainly an important one. Yet working people make this decision every day without even thinking about it as a decision at all.

Other kinds of decisions are hard. They can be hard for two reasons:

1. The decision itself is hard to make. You don't have all the facts. Or you can't be sure of what will happen if you decide a certain way. Or you may want something but not be able to afford it.

2. The decision is hard to carry out. A decision to change a bad habit can be easy to make but hard to put into effect.

What's Your Decision-Making Style?

Understanding your own decision-making style will help you to improve your skills. Circle the answers that tell how you make decisions.

When Faced With A Decision I	#1	#2	#3
1. Put it off until the last minute, or until it is too late.	(usually)	sometimes	hardly ever
2. Ask others what they think, and then make my own decision.	hardly ever	sometimes	(usually)
3. Make the decision before I have enough information.	(usually)	sometimes	hardly ever
4. Do what my friends want me to do.	usually	sometimes	(hardly ever)
5. Do the opposite of what others tell me to do.	usually	sometimes	(hardly ever)
6. Know that I can change my mind if I'm not satisfied with my decision.	hardly ever	(sometimes)	usually
7. Feel confident that I can make a good decision.	hardly ever	(sometimes)	usually
8. Follow-through on my decision once it is made.	hardly ever	(sometimes)	usually
9. Consider all the choices or options.	(hardly ever)	sometimes	usually
10. Choose the first thing I think of.	(usually)	sometimes	hardly ever
11. Feel nervous and anxious.	(usually)	sometimes	hardly ever
12. Think about what could happen as a result of my decision.	(hardly ever)	sometimes	hardly ever

Scoring Yourself: Did you circle any "1"s? If you did, you need to improve in those areas.

Types of Decision Makers

A. **Delayer**—Puts off making decisions, often until it is too late.

B. **Pushover**—Does'nt want to take responsibility for making decisions. This person asks others to do the deciding.

C. **Flip-of-the-Coin**—Leaves decisions to chance, or luck, or doesn't decide at all.

D. **Easy-Way-Out**—Always chooses the easiest way to do something, even if it's not the best way.

E. **Planner**—Has a plan for making decisions.

SITUATION:

Since Fred does not have a car, he rides to work with Joan. Joan has just found a job in another state and will be quitting in two weeks. This means Fred will have to decide how to get to his job after Joan leaves. Some of the decisions he could make are listed below. Match these decisions with the types of decision-makers above. (A,B,C,D,E).

_____ Fred immediately decides the easiest thing to do is to wait for Joan to find him another ride.

_____ After waiting until Joan's last day at work, Fred starts asking around for a ride.

_____ Fred doesn't want to be blamed if he makes a bad decision, so he asks the boss if she thinks he should buy a used car.

_____ Fred makes a list of possible ways to get to work and sets timelines for following these up.

_____ Fred figures there's a chance that Joan's job might fall through, or something will come along to solve the problem for him.

The Decision-Making Process

Careful planning will help you make better decisions. At first this might seem difficult, but after awhile it will seem natural. You will have better control of your life and be a valued employee.

The steps you need to follow are listed below. The activities on the following pages will show you how to use these steps when making decisions.

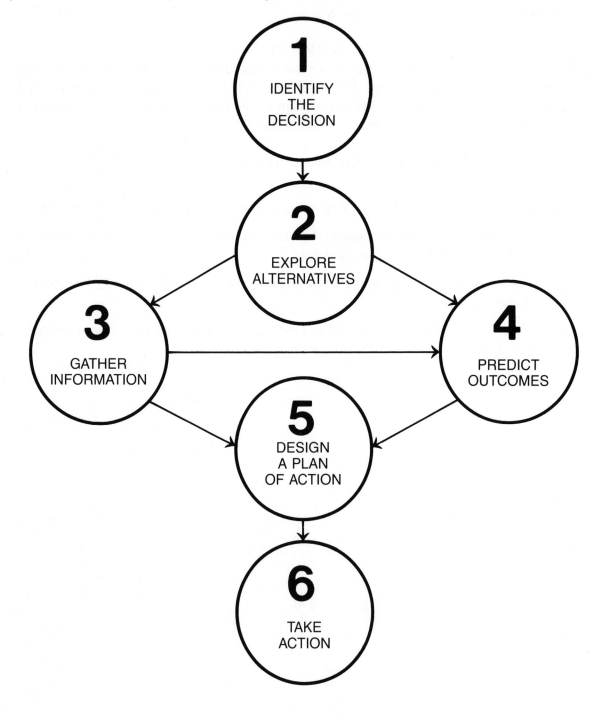

Identifying the decision to be made is the first step in the decision-making process. It is also a very important step. If you aren't sure what the decision is about, you won't be able to begin deciding.

When identifying the decision, you should specify what needs to happen, *not* just what the problem is. This will give you a direction to follow when completing the decision-making steps. For example, suppose Fred stated his situation like this:

"Joan is quitting work."

Although this states the problem, it doesn't identify the decision. It does not state what needs to happen.

Fred should state his situation like this:

"I have to find a new way to get to work in two weeks."

The need for a decision does not have to be based on a negative situation. Perhaps you are invited to two parties on the same day. Your problem is not the fact that you were invited to two parties. It's fun being well-liked. Your problem is deciding which party to go to.

Identify a decision you will have to make soon or that you have faced in the past. Identify the decision to be made.

"I have to _____

_____

_____."

Exploring Alternatives

Some people make poor decisions because they do not think of all the possible solutions or choices they have. The best way to do this is to make a list of as many alternatives as you can. Don't think about whether they are good or bad ideas at first. Just let your imagination go. You can always cross off the ideas you don't like at a later time.

Look at Fred's list of all the alternatives he has for finding a way to work. Then cross off those that you think would not be good solutions.

1. Take the bus.
2. Buy a car.
3. Walk.
4. Hitchhike.
5. Take the train.
6. Borrow a car.
7. Go by skateboard.
8. Try to get a ride with someone else at work.
9. Take a taxi.
10. Quit this job and try to find a closer one.
11. Call the boss for a ride.
12. Put an ad in the paper for car pools.
13. Hope someone offers me a ride.
14. Take a helicopter.
15. Ride a bike.

Now look at the situation below. Make a list of all the possible alternatives for this problem.

Jerry works in a small mailroom. Barb, a co-worker, smokes constantly. Jerry can't stand the smoke. It gives him a headache and makes his eyes water. Jerry is afraid that Barb will get angry or have hurt feelings if he asks her to stop smoking. What are Jerry's alternatives?

1. _____
2. _____
3. _____
4. _____
5. _____
6. _____
7. _____
8. _____
9. _____
10. _____

Gathering Information

Once you have a list of alternatives to choose from, you may need to find out more about each one. For example, Fred's first alternative listed is to TAKE THE BUS. The information Fred would need before choosing this alternative, would be: (1) bus schedule (2) bus route and (3) bus fare.

When gathering information, however, be sure that you have enough information and that it is reliable. Fred made some good and poor decisions based on information he gathered. Place an X in front of each statement that shows poor use of information.

_____ 1. Fred decides to hitchhike because a friend tells him that the police won't bother him.

_____ 2. By calling the taxi service, Fred learns that it will cost too much to get to his job. He decides not to take a taxi.

_____ 3. Three years ago Fred took the bus and his wallet was stolen. He decides not to take the bus.

_____ 4. Fred looks in the want-ads and finds there are no closer jobs available. He decides to keep his job.

_____ 5. Fred decides not to buy a used car because his friend bought a used car and it doesn't work right.

_____ 6. Sal, a co-worker, offers Fred a ride. Judy tells Fred that Sal drives like a maniac and has had several accidents. Fred decides not to ride with Sal.

_____ 7. Fred missed the train the first day because he looked at an old train schedule. He decides not to take a train.

_____ 8. After calling the newspaper, Fred decides to place an ad for car pools. The ad will cost him $3.50 for three days.

Predicting Outcomes

When making a decision, we need to think about what will happen as a result of our actions. Predicting the outcomes or consequences will help in choosing an alternative that is right for you. When we think about the consequences or outcomes, we're thinking about things that *might* or *could* happen. This doesn't always mean that they *will* happen.

Match Fred's alternatives below with the possible outcomes. Note that many of the alternatives have more than one possible outcome.

Alternatives	**Possible Outcomes**
_____ 1. take the bus	A. get picked up by the police
_____ 2. buy a car	B. if I can't find another job, I end up broke
_____ 3. walk	C. meet a new group of people
_____ 4. hitchhike	D. be too tired to work by the time I get there
_____ 5. take the train	E. relax and do some reading on the way to work
_____ 6. borrow a car	
_____ 7. try to get a ride with someone else at work	F. end up with no ride
_____ 8. take a taxi	G. might have to leave earlier, depending on schedules
_____ 9. quit the job and look for a closer one	H. worry about having an accident with someone else's car
_____ 10. call the boss for a ride	I. get into debt, but feel more independent
_____ 11. put an ad in the paper for car pools	J. end up spending a lot of money every day
_____ 12. hope someone offers me a ride	K. develop a friendship with a co-worker
_____ 13. ride a bike	L. get the boss angry
	M. uncomfortable or impossible in very cold, snowy weather or in heavy rains or fogs

Designing a Plan of Action

Once you've made a decision, you're only half done. Next, you need a plan to make your decision work. Look at the alternatives that Fred has listed. If you were Fred, which alternative would you choose first? Choose one that you think would be a good solution. Using the form below, design a plan of action for Fred.

1. take the bus
2. buy a car
3. walk
4. hitchhike
5. take the train
6. borrow a car
7. take a skateboard
8. try to get a ride with someone else at work
9. take a taxi
10. quit this job and try to find a closer one
11. call the boss for a ride
12. put an ad in the paper for car pools
13. hope someone offers me a ride
14. take a helicopter

Plan of Action for Fred

What am I going to do?_____

_____

When will I start?_____

_____

How will I do this?_____

_____

What problems might I have?_____

_____

What is my alternate plan?_____

_____

_____

Now that you've helped Fred solve his problem, it's time to look at yourself.

Below is a list of job-related decisions which people face. Think about decisions you might face on a job. Add them to this list.

1. Should I change jobs?

2. Should I quit my job?

3. How should I act towards the new supervisor?

4. Should I date a co-worker or my boss?

5. Should I take this promotion that's been offered to me?

6. How should I handle the problem I'm having with a co-worker (or the boss)?

7. Should I bring my lunch or eat out at a fast-food place?

8. What should I do about the joker at work who keeps putting me down?

9. When the smoking bothers me, what should I do?

10. When should I ask for vacation time?

11. When people are gossiping about co-workers or the boss, what should I do?

12. Should I ask for a raise?

13. _____

14. _____

15. _____

16. _____

17. _____

18. _____

19. _____

20. _____

Making Your Own Decisions

Think of a decision you have to make in the near future. Use the one you wrote down in the exercise called "Identify the Decision" or think of another one. Write it down:

1. **Decision to be made:** _____

_____

_____

Now fill out the chart:

2. **Alternatives** (What possible solutions or choices do I have?)	3. **Information** (What information do I need about the alternatives?)	4. **Possible outcomes or consequences** (What might happen if I do this?)
a. _____ _____	a. _____ _____	a. _____ _____
b. _____ _____	b. _____ _____	b. _____ _____
c. _____ _____	c. _____ _____	c. _____ _____
d. _____ _____	d. _____ _____	d. _____ _____
e. _____ _____	e. _____ _____	e. _____ _____
f. _____ _____	f. _____ _____	f. _____ _____
g. _____ _____	g. _____ _____	g. _____ _____

5. **Plan of Action:**

What am I going to do? _____

When will I start? _____

How will I do this?_____

What problems might I have?_____

What is my alternate plan?_____

6. **Take Action:**

Begin your plan on the date you stated in #5. What will be your first step?_____

_____

Report back to the class how your decision turned out.

9. STRESS

Stress is an unpleasant feeling of being under pressure. You can feel stress if you're angry, or worried, or keyed up for action, or in a hurry. Many things in daily life can cause you to be under stress.

Stress on the job can be a major problem. No one can avoid it. Everyone should try to learn how to handle it. If you can handle stress on the job, your work life will be much more pleasant and productive than if stress constantly gets you down.

This section of the book will give you some insights into how you can handle stress.

How Does Stress Make You Feel?

Mary King works at Johnson's Drugstore. One of her responsibilities this week is to open the store at 8:00 a.m., since the owner is on vacation. She has the only key.

At 7:30 a.m., when she tried to start her car, the battery was dead. She immediately called her service station. They told her it would be at least an hour before they could start her car.

Mary is frustrated and angry. She would like to take a hammer to her car. She can feel a headache coming on.

If you were Mary, would you feel the same way she does? If not, how would you feel?

_____

_____

_____

If you were Mary, what would you do? _____

_____

_____

_____

Ken Gonzalez has been named top salesperson of the year by Cozy Home Realty. He is getting an award tonight from his company and the Indian Valley Board of Realtors. He has been nervous all day.

Now, as he sits at the banquet, he can feel his heart pounding. He wonders, half seriously, if he is going to have a heart attack. He wishes he were a million miles away.

If you were Ken, would you feel the same way that he does? If not, how would you feel?

_____

_____

_____

If you were Ken, what would you do? _____

_____

_____

_____

Stressful Feelings

Both Mary and Ken are experiencing stress. They feel tension in their bodies. There are a number of things that can be learned from their stories:

1. Stress can be caused by both positive and negative events. Negative: Mary's car would not start. Positive: Ken won an award.

2. Under stress the first reaction for most people is to: a.) get angry or want to fight back; or b.) run away from the situation. Mary wanted to attack her car. Ken wanted to leave the banquet.

3. Each person reacts differently to stressful situations. Mary was starting to have a headache. Ken's heart was pounding.

4. What is highly stressful for one person may involve little or no stress for another. If you were Mary, you may not have been very upset. If you were Ken, you may have enjoyed getting an award.

Everyone at some time or another has feelings similar to Mary's and Ken's on the job. They may be labeled in different ways: tension, nervousness, depression. All are a result of stress. Here are some of the other common ways people feel and act under stress.

angry	muscle stiffness	running away
fearful	pounding heart	yelling
irritable	shortness of breath	panic
indecisive	general aches and pains	crying
too sensitive	upset stomach	eating
jumpy	dizziness	fighting
tired	can't sleep	confused
depressed	nausea	headache

Think of the last time you were under stress at work. If you do not have a job, think of the last time you were under stress at school or at home. From the list above choose the ways that you felt and acted. Write them below:

1. _____   4. _____

2. _____   5. _____

3. _____   6. _____

How Do Stressful Situations Affect Job Performance?

1. You are working as a salesperson in a large department store. As you are standing at the cash register, a customer comes up and says that you shortchanged him. He is angry and says that this has happened to him before.

   Would you feel stress in this situation? _____

   If so, how would the feeling of stress affect what you would do? _____

   _____

   _____

   _____

   _____

   What **would** you do? _____

   _____

   _____

   _____

   _____

2. Your employer came up after work and told you she wanted to recommend you as worker of the month. You don't feel you deserve the award since you know you've made many mistakes on the job.

   Would you feel stress in this situation? _____

   If so, how would the feeling of stress affect what you would do? _____

   _____

   _____

   _____

   What **would** you do? _____

   _____

   _____

   _____

   _____

3. Your supervisor has told you to deliver some packages across town. He gave you directions and you wrote them down. Somehow you have taken a wrong turn. You find yourself hopelessly lost and confused.

Would you feel stress in this situation? _____

If so, how would the feeling of stress affect what you would do? _____

_____

_____

_____

What **would** you do? _____

_____

_____

_____

_____

4. You have been offered a promotion. It would mean better pay; but it would require longer hours and more responsibility. You would also become the supervisor of your co-workers, many of whom are also your friends.

Would you feel stress in this situation? _____

If so, how would the feeling of stress affect what you would do? _____

_____

_____

_____

What **would** you do? _____

_____

_____

_____

_____

5. You and some co-workers get together after work. They begin to gossip about one of your supervisors, Miss Johnson. You like and respect her; but you also want to get along with your friends.

Would you feel stress in this situation? _____

If so, how would the feeling of stress affect what you would do? _____

_____

_____

_____

What **would** you do? _____

_____

_____

_____

_____

Check the columns that tell how you feel and act at work or in school.

How I feel and act:	Often	Sometimes	Hardly Ever
I am physically tired			
I am emotionally tired			
I am unhappy			
I have headaches			
I am worried			
I am angry			
I feel rejected			
I am depressed			
I cry easily			
I'm too sensitive			
I'm irritable			
I'm tense			
I get into fights			
I'm jumpy, always moving			
I can't concentrate			
I can't sleep			
I have an upset stomach			
I'm nervous			

To score yourself, turn the page upside down.

Scoring yourself: If you have checked three or more in the "OFTEN" column, you seem to be under a lot of stress at work or in school. Discover the causes in the next few pages and begin to work on it.

Causes of Stress

It is important to understand what things in your work—either at school or on a job—are causing you problems. Once you know them, you can begin to make plans to change yourself or the situation. Put a check in front of any items that cause you stress.

Personal:

_____ I don't feel I'm a very good worker.

_____ I am always behind with my work.

_____ I dislike my job (or going to school).

_____ There are other things I'd like to do at work (or school).

_____ I don't get enough exercise.

_____ I don't have a healthy diet.

_____ I have no important interests outside of my job (or school).

_____ Other: _____

Other people:

_____ Other people are favored over me.

_____ I have problems with supervisors (or teachers).

_____ I don't like some of my co-workers (or school mates).

_____ I am uncomfortable working with others.

_____ I am always fighting with someone.

_____ I am criticized too often.

_____ No one ever helps me.

_____ I am criticized in public.

_____ I get blamed when others don't do their job.

_____ Other: _____

Your place of work (or classroom):

_____ I don't like it because of the poor conditions (dirt, noise, temperature, lighting).

_____ I don't have enough authority or responsibility.

_____ I have too much work to do.

_____ I always have the same kind of thing to do.

_____ I am always being asked to start a new task before the old one is finished.

_____ Other: _____

How Do You Handle Stress?

Take a look at the way you usually act under stress. Go back to your causes of stress in the last exercise and write six of them below. If you do not have six, write as many as you can.

When you are finished, look at the opposite column (RESPONSE STYLE). Match your RESPONSE STYLE with your STRESSFUL SITUATION. It is all right to use the same response style more than once. An example is given below.

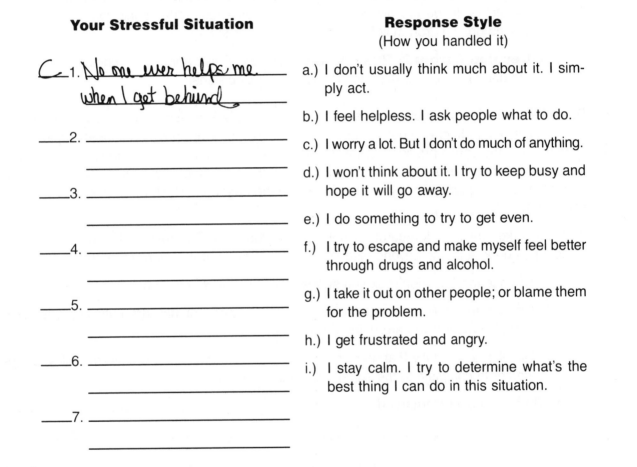

Your Stressful Situation

C 1. No one ever helps me. when I get behind

___2. ___

___3. ___

___4. ___

___5. ___

___6. ___

___7. ___

Response Style
(How you handled it)

a.) I don't usually think much about it. I simply act.

b.) I feel helpless. I ask people what to do.

c.) I worry a lot. But I don't do much of anything.

d.) I won't think about it. I try to keep busy and hope it will go away.

e.) I do something to try to get even.

f.) I try to escape and make myself feel better through drugs and alcohol.

g.) I take it out on other people; or blame them for the problem.

h.) I get frustrated and angry.

i.) I stay calm. I try to determine what's the best thing I can do in this situation.

Once you have identified your sources of stress, the next question is: What can I do about it? There are three different approaches:

1. **Change the Situation.** Get rid of whatever is causing you stress. If you feel you are being unfairly blamed when others don't do their job, talk with your supervisor.

2. **Change the Way You Look at Things.** Sometimes a new look at things removes the stress. If you are always assigned the same task, don't think your supervisor is picking on you. You may be the best person for the job.

3. **Develop Carefully Planned Responses.** Think about your choices and follow the decision-making steps in the section on Decisions.

Read the stories below. Circle the answer that best describes what you think the person should do in this situation. If you do not like any of the choices, or if you have additional suggestions, write them in the space provided. (Hint: Think all three approaches over carefully. "Develop a Carefully Planned Response" may not always be the best approach. Or it may be a good approach, but the particular response may not be the best one. Think through each response carefully!)

A. A co-worker criticizes Margaret for not doing a good job. She resents it. She feels she is doing as good a job as anyone else. What would you do it you were Margaret?

1. Change the Situation: Ask you supbervisor to change your job.

2. Change the Way You Look at Things: Your supervisor has not criticized you. This probably means you are doing a good job.

3. Develop a Carefully Planned Response: The next time you are criticized tell your co-worker to complain to the supervisor and not to you.

What else could Margaret do? _____

_____

_____

B. Bill has been working at the same job for three years. His supervisor has often told him that he is doing a good job. Yet, other workers hired after him have been promoted. He does not understand why he has been passed by. What would you do it you were Bill?

1. Change the Situation: Look for a new job.

2. Change the Way You Look at Things: Ask yourself if you really want a promotion. It may mean more money; but also longer hours, more responsibility and supervision of coworkers.

3. Develop a Carefully Planned Response: Go to your supervisor and ask why you have not been promoted.

What else could Bill do? _____

_____

_____

C. Norma feels she is always behind in her work. She asks herself: "Am I being given too much work, or am I too slow to handle it?" What would you do it you were Norma?

　　1. Change the Situation: Decide which are the most important tasks and get those done first.

　　2. Change the Way You Look at Things: Tell yourself you are doing the best you can. Don't worry about the tasks you cannot do.

　　3. Develop a Carefully Planned Response: Ask your supervisor for a list of your job tasks and responsibilities. If you have been given extra work to do, tell your supervisor. Perhaps some of your tasks and responsibilities can be given to others.

　　What else could Norma do? _____

_____

_____

D. Mike often finds himself arguing with his co-workers. He does not think it is his fault. However, a friend of his has told him that his supervisor has noticed the arguing. What would you do it you were Mike?

　　1. Change the Situation: Try to avoid those co-workers with whom you are having trouble.

　　2. Change the Way You Look at Things: Realize that most of the things you are arguing about are not important. If it is important, discuss it with your supervisor.

　　3. Develop a Carefully Planned Response: Begin a program of moderate daily exercise to work off your tension.

　　What else could Mike do? _____

_____

_____

E. Mary's supervisor in a retail store criticizes her in public for not keeping her merchandise neat and orderly. Mary is very hurt and embarrassed. What would you do if you were Mary?

　　1. Change the Situation: Ask for a transfer to a new department and a new supervisor.

2. Change the Way You Look at Things: Even though this is a poor way to handle the problem, realize this is the way the supervisor gets things done.

3. Develop a Carefully Planned Response: Ask the supervisor for a private conference if it ever happens again.

What else could Mary do? _____

_____

_____

F. Rosanne does an excellent job when working alone. When she works with others, however, she becomes tense and irritable. What would you do if you were Rosanne?

1. Change the Situation: Ask your supervisor to assign you to tasks in which you can work alone.

2. Change the Way You Look at Things: Realize that your co-workers are nice people who may be able to help you do a better job.

3. Develop a Carefully Planned Response: To lessen the effects of stress, make sure you have a well-balanced and nutritious diet.

What else could Rosanne do? _____

_____

_____

G. Kevin has been with the same company for five years. He has noticed that many workers who have been with the company three or four years are being laid off. Since his company does not seem to be doing much business, he is worried about keeping his job. What would you do if you were Kevin?

1. Change the Situation: Go to a job placement agency and begin looking for a new job.

2. Change the Way You Look at Things: Worry is not going to solve the problem. Some workers hired only a year or two ago still have their jobs.

3. Develop a Carefully Planned Response: Talk over the situation with your supervisor. If you are still not certain after this conference, begin to look for a new job.

What else could Kevin do? _____

_____

_____

Identify a stressful situation that you are experiencing at the present time on the job. If you are not working, then choose one from your personal, home, or social life.

1. Describe the stressful situation as clearly as you can: _____

_____

_____

_____

_____

_____

2. What could you do now to make the situation you described above less stressful? Choose one of the three approaches listed below. Tell how you would use this approach to make the situation less stressful.

a. Change the Situation: _____

_____

_____

_____

b. Change the Way you Look at Things: _____

_____

_____

_____

c. Develop a Carefully Planned Response: _____

_____

_____

_____

_____

_____

_____

Stress and Daily Habits

Single incidents or specific problems like the ones described in this chapter are not the only causes of stress. Certain habits or patterns of daily life can be very stressful in themselves. And many habit patterns can make you more susceptible to stress from outside incidents.

Check any of the following that apply to you:

_____ 1. I eat desserts and candy regularly. I drink soft drinks regularly, too.

_____ 2. I drink several cups of coffee or tea every day, or cola drinks.

_____ 3. I don't get much regular exercise; I don't play sports regularly.

_____ 4. I smoke cigarettes.

_____ 5. I could use more sleep at night.

_____ 6. I don't go on trips or vacations.

_____ 7. I eat lots of canned or processed foods.

_____ 8. I watch lots of adventure shows on TV.

_____ 9. I don't have any hobbies or strong interests.

_____ 10. I'm often bored.

Every one of the above is associated with stress for some people. The more items you checked, the more likely you are to be the victim of stress.

Desserts, soft drinks, and candy are loaded with sugar, which many people cannot tolerate in large amounts. Too much sugar makes them tense and jumpy.

Coffee, tea, and cola drinks contain the drug caffeine. It can stimulate you, and let you down with a crash.

Sports and exercise give you an opportunity to work off tensions and keep you in good shape.

People who smoke are harming their bodies, and frequently feel under tension. The drug nicotine in tobacco can add to the jumpy feeling.

Sleep lets you relax after tensions.

Trips and vacations offer a change of pace, a chance to get away from daily stresses.

Canned and processed foods contain chemicals that make some people tense and nervous.

A constant diet of adventure shows and violence has been shown to raise most people's stress levels.

Hobbies and outside interests offer a chance for relaxation and enjoyment.

Boredom shows you don't have enough interesting things in your life. Stresses will get to you more with nothing to take your mind off them.

10. INITIATIVE

Initiative means doing what should be done without being told to do it.

When you *initiate* something, it means you start it. Some one who comes up with new ideas, who solves small problems on the job without looking for help or direction, who can be trusted to work on his or her own, is showing initiative.

Initiative is an enormously valuable trait in a worker. The worker who shows initiative will do better work and enjoy the job more than one who must be led and directed all the time.

Initiative includes all of the following:
1. Showing willingness to work (not just putting your time in, or just "punching the clock");
2. Keeping busy in your place of work;
3. Doing extra work when needed;
4. Putting in extra time if it helps get the work done;
5. Helping others in their work, if needed;
6. Presenting a new and better way to get the job done;
7. Taking courses or subjects that improve job performance.

Initiative starts with knowing what your job tasks are. There is no point in doing extra work until you're doing your regular job well.

Read the description below:

JOB DESCRIPTION

JOB TITLE: Shipping Clerk

DEPARTMENT: Shipping

GENERAL SUMMARY OF RESPONSIBILITY:

Prepare merchandise and products for shipping. Responsible for merchandise being received in good condition. Keep records of shipments sent out and received.

SPECIFIC JOB RESPONSIBILITIES:

1. Requests merchandise from supply room
2. Checks correctness of orders
3. Packs goods for shipping
4. Determines least expensive and quickest method of shipping
5. Keeps records of weight, cost, dates, and methods of shipment for each order.

If you are working, write your own description in the space below. If you are not working, write a description for a position for which you have applied, or for one you would like to have. Or interview a friend who is working and write down her or his job description.

JOB DESCRIPTION

JOB TITLE:_____

GENERAL SUMMARY OF RESPONSIBILITY:_____

_____

_____

SPECIFIC JOB RESPONSIBILITIES:

1. _____

   _____

2. _____

   _____

3. _____

   _____

4. _____

   _____

5. _____

   _____

WAYS TO SHOW INITIATIVE. There are many ways to show initiative. Below is a list of some of the ways.

     Help another worker when your work is done.
     Help the boss get his/her work done.
     Ask your boss for more work to do.
     Suggest a new way to do your work more efficiently.

Using the job description you wrote on the previous page, list some specific ways you might show initiative on this particular job. (You might want to ask your boss to help you develop this list.)

_____

_____

_____

_____

How Do Others Show Initiative on the Job?

Interview three people who are employed. Find out how they or their co-workers show initiative at their place of work.

Put the results of your interview below.

Job Title	Ways to Show Initiative
1. _____	1. _____ _____ 2. _____ _____ 3. _____ _____
2. _____	1. _____ _____ 2. _____ _____ 3. _____ _____
3. _____	1. _____ _____ 2. _____ _____ 3. _____ _____

Initiative Has Its Benefits

Susan is the Business Department Manager at Supreme Chemical Company. Among her many tasks is the responsibility of putting all money away in the safe at the end of the day. In addition, she has to secure the area, which means to lock all doors and turn out the main lights.

One Friday afternoon, she was suddenly called home because of a family emergency. Juan, a secretary in the Personnel Department, noticed as he was leaving the building, that the money was still left out in the office. Before leaving, Juan put the money in the safe, locked the doors and turned out the main lights.

1. In what way did Juan show initiative? _____

_____

_____

_____

2. How will his initiative benefit Susan? _____

_____

_____

_____

3. How will his initiative benefit the entire Business Department? _____

_____

_____

_____

4. How will Juan benefit by showing initiative? _____

_____

_____

_____

5. How will Juan's initiative benefit the Personnel Department even though he helped the

Business Department? _____

_____

_____

_____

Do You Show Initiative on the Job?

Do you show initiative on the job? Or, if you don't have a job yet, do you have personality characteristics that suggest that you would show initiative on a job?

To get an idea of how you stand, fill out the chart below. Follow these directions:

IF YOU HAVE A JOB: simply fill out the chart as is, using the rating system shown.

IF YOU DON'T HAVE A JOB: Think of settings where effort or work is expected of you. For example, at home, where house or yard chores need to be done. Or at school or in your school work. Or work on a hobby or other fun activity, especially one where you interact with other people.

Pick one such setting and describe it briefly here: _____

_____

_____

Now fill out the initiative chart below:

5 = Excellent   4 = Good   3 = Average   2 = Below Average   1 = Needs Much Improvement

Initiative Item	5	4	3	2	1
A. Willing to work (not just put in time)					
B. Helping others on the job					
C. Keeping busy (when my regular job is done)					
D. Doing extra work when needed					
E. Putting in extra time (if needed)					
F. Doing positive things to help improve the spirit of the company.					
G. Taking courses or subjects that improve my job performance					
H. Suggesting new and better ways to improve job performance					

If convenient, have someone else look at your chart and see if they would grade it the same way.

Initiative Can Help You Promote Yourself!

Showing initiative can lead to job promotion and, in some cases, to bonuses.

Pretend you are the Head Supervisor of the Physical Therapy Unit of Good Shepherd Hospital. The Personnel Department Manager has told you that you may promote two people in your department to supervisory positions. She has also given you $1,000 bonus money to distribute among the workers on the basis of how well they have shown initiative. The total amount that you distribute cannot total, among all workers, more than $1,000. An individual employee may get any amount from $0 to $1,000.

Read the descriptions below. Decide on whom you would promote and then distribute the bonus money.

Physical Therapy Unit, Good Shepherd Hospital

Linda: Works overtime when asked. Often helps patients on her own time. Does not participate in company social activities.

Ruta: Seldom has to be told what to do. Has missed work often but usually because of family problems. Her absence irritates co-workers. She enrolled at a local community college in a 2-year program which will qualify her for a higher position in physical therapy.

Tom: Works very well alone on the job. Usually does not help other co-workers except when asked. He has thought of new ways to get the job done more efficiently.

Pedro: Does not "watch the clock." If the job requires extra hours, he puts the time in. He is thinking of looking for a higher-paying job at another hospital.

Alma: Gets along very well with co-workers, but has quite a few disagreements with her supervisors. Volunteers to come in on her day off if the hospital needs her.

Indicate below whom you would or would not promote. Then distribute the $1000 to the workers according to how well they have shown initiative. Keep in mind that you may want to promote different people from the ones you give the highest bonuses to.

	Promote?	Why/Why Not?	Bonus Money Given
Linda			
Ruta			
Tom			
Pedro			
Alma			

11. GOAL SETTING

If you are to get the most out of your job, you will have to do it well. You'll need to take a close look at the Job Survival Skills that this book deals with. And you'll have to look for ways to improve your own Job Survival Skills.

To do this, you have to set goals for yourself. You have to identify the skills that you need to work on, and design a program for yourself to reach the level of improvement you set for yourself.

This chapter will show you a 5-step way to set goals and reach them:

1. Set a specific goal.

2. Plan ways to achieve your goal.

3. Identify any obstacles.

4. Overcome obstacles.

5. Evaluate your progress.

Setting a Specific Goal

To start off, determine what you are going to do and when you are going to do it.

This means, first of all, that you must set a goal that is very specific. The more specific the goal, the easier it is to know if you have reached it.

For example, Fred works at the Customer Service Desk for Stills Department Store. When asked by his supervisor to set his number one goal for the coming month, Fred wrote:

"I will deal more effectively with the public."

The supervisor responded by saying that that goal was too general. She noticed that Fred has had a problem dealing with the angry customer. She specified the following goal for Fred:

"You will listen carefully to the complaints of the angry customers. You won't argue with them."

Below are a number of goals involving Job Survival Skills. After each one, check whether you think it is specific too general. If you rate it as too general, rewrite it to be more specific in the space provided. (Leave the space blank if you think the goal is specific enough.)

1. "I will communicate better with others on the job." ☐ specific ☐ too general

   _____

   _____

   _____

2. "I will answer all telephone calls before they ring three times." ☐ specific ☐ too general

   _____

   _____

   _____

3. "I will reduce my stress at work by looking at things in a different way." ☐ specific ☐ too general

   _____

   _____

   _____

4. "I will show more initiative at work." ☐ specific ☐ too general

   _____

   _____

   _____

Plan Ways to Achieve Your Goal

The second step in reaching your goal is to plan the ways in which you will accomplish it. In Fred's situation, he decided that he would listen more effectively.

He would do this by:
    a. looking at the eyes of the other person
    b. nodding his head
    c. using facial expressions that show interest and concern

Can you think of other ways that Fred could show he is listening more carefully to the angry customer? List them below:

_____

_____

_____

Complete the sentences below. For each sentence, list three ways to accomplish the goal. Some are already listed for you.

1. I will communicate better with others by

    1. offering supportive statements;

    2. improving my personal appearance;

    3. _____

2. I will establish a budget in order to manage my money better by

    1. obtaining a budget form and keeping a record of payments and receipts;

    2. _____

    3. _____

3. I will make better decisions by

    1. _____

    2. _____

    3. _____

Identify Obstacles and Mind Binders

Many times you set goals and enthusiastically start on your way to achieve them. Then, obstacles come up which you must overcome if you are going to reach your goal.

For Fred, the main obstacle was his short temper. He would start getting angry when the customer would complain about poor service or a poor product. This is a real obstacle.

Mind Binders are another type of obstacle—a false obstacle. Mind Binders are excuses—things you tell yourself that keep you from reaching your goal. It's important to recognize Mind Binders if you are using them.

In Column B are Mind Binder statements. Match those statements with the Goal Areas listed in Column A. The first two are done for you.

Column A	**Column B**
Goal Areas	Mind Binders
_4_ A. telephone courtesy	1. "What's going to happen is going to happen anyway."
_5_ B. attendance	2. "I'm not paid to try extra hard, so why should I?"
___ C. communication	3. "I really can't afford to buy new clothes."
___ D. decision-making	4. "People talk too fast on the phone so I can't always get the full message."
___ E. cooperation with employer	5. "My alarm clock doesn't ring loud enough so I don't hear it in the morning."
___ F. personal grooming	6. "I've never been good with numbers."
___ G. dealing with the public	7. "I don't mind dealing with adults; the little children drive me crazy."
___ H. initiative	8. "I'll always have trouble with worrying too much."
___ I. cooperation with co-workers	9. "I just can't get along with loud people."
___ J. money management	10. "I can't listen when it's so noisy."
___ K. stress management	11. "I don't think I'll ever figure out what my boss really wants from me."

Overcome Obstacles

When Mind Binders or other obstacles come between you and your goal, use the following steps to overcome the obstacles:

1. Identify the obstacle. Once you have taken time to identify what the obstacle is, then your problem is half-solved.

2. Consider all possible solutions. Think of all the possible ways to overcome the obstacle.

Fred found out that his main obstacle was his short temper. To overcome that obstacle, he considers the following solutions:

a. When dealing with a customer, he will ask the supervisor or another employee to help out if his temper is close to exploding.

b. He will ask someone he respects for advice on how to control his temper.

c. He will listen very attentively to what the customer is saying and find a way to solve the customer's problem.

Of the possible solutions Fred considered, which one or ones would you choose if you were Fred? Why?_____

_____

_____

Read the situation below and then answer the questions.

A. Amelda has set a goal of communicating more effectively with her boss, Pedro. She has been asking for extra work. She goes out of her way to be friendly with Pedro. However, Pedro is a Quiet Boss and doesn't talk much. Amelda has become very frustrated in her attempt to reach her goal.

Identify Amelda's obstacle:_____

_____

List some possible solutions Amelda might consider in overcoming her obstacle.

_____

_____

_____

It's important to know when you're making progress or when you've reached your goal. For Fred, the proof came when his supervisor wrote on his evaluation form:

"Fred has improved in dealing with angry customers. He seldom gets upset, and he listens carefully to their complaints."

A supervisor's comment may be one way to evaluate your progress. Some other ways are listed in the exercises below. When you set up an evaluation standard for your progress, keep in mind the following points:

- Don't confuse signs of progress on the way to your goal with finally reaching your goal. Part way there isn't the same as all the way there. Don't slack off when you're part way there.

- Be careful of opinions you ask for from others. Your friends don't want to hurt your feelings. They may tell you only what they think you want to hear.

- Be careful about asking your boss for evaluations on your progress, unless he or she has brought up the problem in the first place. If your boss hasn't yet noticed that you are late too often, don't tell him or her. Improve on your own.

- Don't set unrealistic goals or impossibly high standards. If you have been dressing messily, for example, don't demand of yourself that you dress like a fashion plate immediately.

- Don't set your sights too low, either. Demand of yourself that you show real signs of improvement.

In the exercise below, check each evaluation that you think is a good way to measure progress of the goal listed above it. Leave blank any evaluation you think is not a good one.

If you think none of the evaluations for a goal are good ones, write in what you would recommend on the line marked "other."

Personal Appearance

Goal: I will dress appropriately for work.

Evaluation:

a. take a picture before I start my goal and a picture after I think I've reached my goal. Compare the two pictures.
b. ask my employer to evaluate how I'm doing in my personal appearance
c. other employees tell me that I look better without my asking them

d. other: _____

Dealing with the Public

Goal: I will follow rules for dealing with the public set down by the company.

Evaluation:

      a. show the boss a list of how many courtesy rules I followed on a certain day
      b. win my company's courtesy award
      c. listen to a tape that recorded how many times I said, "thank you"

      d. other:_____

Money Management

Goal: I will follow my budget.

Evaluation:

      a. have money left over at the end of the month
      b. all my bills are paid at the end of the month
      c. extra money is available to put in savings at the end of the month

      d. other:_____

Attendance

Goal: I will be at work every day for a month.

Evaluation:

      a. look at my time card
      b. ask employer if I've improved
      c. look at my pay check

      d. other:_____

Initiative

Goal: I will volunteer to help the boss by doing extra work.

Evaluation:

      a. check a list of how many times in a day I have asked the boss if I can do extra work
      b. be selected for promotion
      c. check my evaluation write-up

      d. other:_____